Contents

Who were the Vikings?

The Vikings lived in the cold northern lands of Norway, Sweden and Denmark about 1000 years ago.
Between 800-1100 AD, they ruled over a large territory, including parts of Britain and France.

Today, many people think of the Vikings as brutal raiders, attacking peaceful towns, villages and churches. This is partly true. Viking warriors did sail off on pirate raids in search of rich plunder.

But at home, and in the lands where they settled, the Vikings were also farmers, fishermen, craft-workers, ship-builders, traders and poets. Viking people enjoyed feasting, music and songs. And all free Viking men played a part in running their own village community.

A peaceful procession of Viking people, riding on horseback and in carts. From a Viking tapestry, woven around AD 1000.

FACE to FACE

VIKINGS & SAXONS

Fiona Macdonald

SIMON & SCHUSTER
YOUNG BOOKS

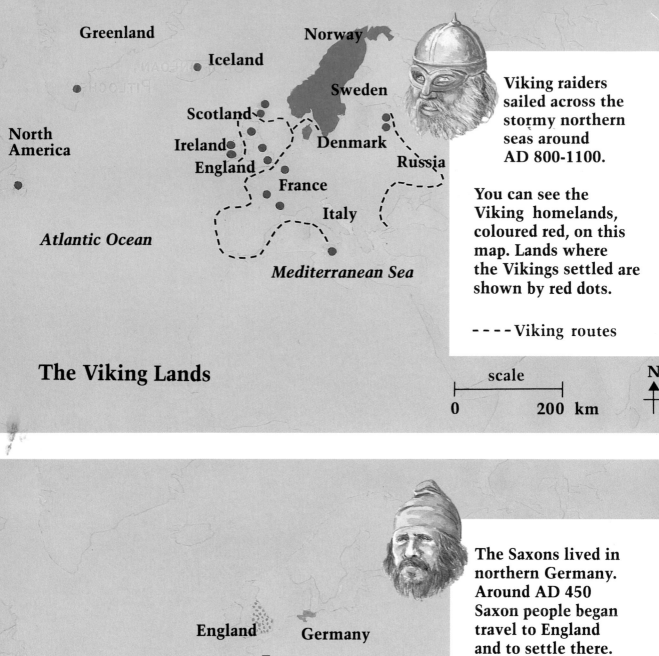

Greenland

Norway

Iceland

Sweden

Scotland

North
America

Ireland

Denmark

England

Russia

France

Atlantic Ocean

Italy

Mediterranean Sea

Viking raiders
sailed across the
stormy northern
seas around
AD 800-1100.

You can see the
Viking homelands,
coloured red, on this
map. Lands where
the Vikings settled are
shown by red dots.

- - - - Viking routes

The Viking Lands

scale

0   200 km

N

England   Germany

France

Atlantic Ocean

Mediterranean Sea

The Saxons lived in
northern Germany.
Around AD 450
Saxon people began
travel to England
and to settle there.

You can see the
Saxon homelands,
coloured green, on this
map. Lands where
the Saxons settled are
shown by green dots.

The Saxon Lands

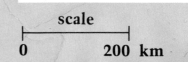

scale

0   200 km

N

This richly-decorated tombstone tells us a lot about Viking beliefs and customs. At the top, we can see a warrior on horseback being welcomed into Valhalla (heaven) by a woman offering him a drink of mead. Vikings believed this happened to the souls of men who died in battle. At the bottom of the tombstone, we can see a typical Viking ship and its warrior crew.

Viking warriors used long, broad swords, spears and battleaxes to attack. These heavy iron swords have survived from Viking times.

Very few portraits of Viking people have survived. This little metal head shows a Viking warrior. It was perhaps made as a good luck charm.

Who were the Saxons?

The Saxons came from the coast lands of northern Germany. They were one of several peoples—Angles, Saxons and Jutes—who had lived there for centuries. They settled in England, because the sea was flooding their fields. The people living in England belonged to Celtic tribes. Some had married Roman soldiers and officials, and copied the Roman way of life. The Romans ruled England for many years, but left in AD 410.

Nobody knows how many Saxons went to England, or exactly when they arrived. But by about AD 500, most of England was ruled by Saxon kings. They made laws, led armies, and collected taxes.

Saxon kings were rich. They loved fine clothes and treasures. This solid gold belt buckle and jewelled war-helmet were found buried at Sutton Hoo in southern England. They probably belonged to the Saxon King Redwald, who died around AD 620.

solid earth bank

workmen with spades

royal official

building supervisor

king's bodyguard

king

A Saxon king visiting a new earthwork—a huge barrier made of stones and soil. It is being built by man-power. There were no big machines in Saxon times.

Earthworks like these marked the boundaries between warring Saxon kingdoms. They were difficult for an army to cross on foot or even on horseback.

wooden posts

wattle and daub walls

thatched roof

village pond

Saxon houses were made of wood, twigs and mud (known as wattle and daub). They were roofed with thatch made of reeds or straw.

Saxon lifestyle

The Saxons were farmers, and lived in villages.
They grew wheat and barley, and kept chickens,
sheep and cows. Women wove thick woollen cloth,
cooked, cleaned and cared for children, also they
worked with the men in the fields.

Wealthy Saxons built large houses, but there were
few Saxon cities. The Saxons were impressed when
they arrived in Britain and saw the remains of
Roman temples in deserted Roman towns.

The Saxons settled mostly in England. Other parts
of Britain—Scotland, Ireland and Wales—kept many
of their old Celtic laws, spoke Celtic languages,
and preserved the Celtic way of life.

**Saxon scribes produced many
fine manuscripts, illustrated
with pictures of everyday life.
This Saxon manuscript shows
a nobleman chasing wild birds
with his specially-trained hawk.**

Viking lifestyle

Life was harsh in the cold Viking homelands. Viking farmers worked hard all summer to grow grain to feed their families in winter. Women gathered wild honey, herbs and berries, brewed beer and made cheese. Men went hunting for bears, seals, rabbits, whales and birds. They caught fish which they preserved by salting and smoking. They trapped foxes and ermine for their soft, thick fur.

Wealthy people used fur to line warm clothes made of fine wool and, sometimes, silk. Ordinary men wore linen shirts, rough woollen cloaks, trousers, and tunics. Women wore linen shifts and long warm dresses fastened with silver brooches. Everyone had leather shoes coated with waterproof grease.

These chessmen were found on the Isle of Lewis, off Scotland. They were made around AD 1100. They are carved from walrus tusks (teeth). They show powerful people in Viking society—a king, a queen and a Viking warrior.

loom for weaving cloth

sheeps' wool

open fire

typical Viking jewels

wooden dish

Viking houses were built of wood, turf (slabs of earth and grass), or stone. They were lined with wooden planks, to help keep them warm. Fires also provided warmth, but made rooms very smoky.

Viking farm

sheltered inlet, called a fjord

ship sailing

Viking boat builders were very skilled. Ships were made of wooden planks, nailed together. They were fast, light and easy to steer.

adze for shaping wood

hammer

carpenter

wedges to split wood

blacksmith making nails

Sailors and explorers

The Vikings were skilful sailors. No-one else owned such well-built ships, or dared travel so far. The Vikings studied navigation, tides, wind and weather. Out at sea, they used the stars and the movements of birds and fish to guide them.

Viking sailors travelled for many reasons—to fight, to raid, to trade or to seek new lands where they could settle. Some Vikings travelled in search of adventure. They made the dangerous journey across the Atlantic Ocean to discover the uninhabited islands of Iceland and Greenland. And a few brave Viking explorers, led by Lief Erikson, reached the North American coast.

This 1000-year-old ship was found buried in Sweden. It is decorated with a tall, curving prow and stern, like the head and tail of a dragon.

It was powered by men rowing, and by a large square sail. This Viking ship is 21.6 metres long and 5 metres wide.

International trade

The Vikings were always looking for plunder, but they were also keen to trade. They knew that Viking timber, furs, walrus ivory, amber and honey would fetch high prices. They also sold prisoners captured in Viking raids, to work as slaves.

Viking merchants travelled vast distances overland to trade in Russia, Turkey and the Middle East. They journeyed through thick forests and along frozen rivers. They met Arab merchants selling silks, spices, jewels, perfumes and fine metalwork.

Trading towns grew up, like Hedeby in Denmark and Birka in Sweden. Viking merchants sold local goods, and rich and rare treasures from distant lands.

These silver coins, decorated with Arabic writing, were found in the Viking lands. They show that Viking merchants traded with people from the Middle East.

Viking merchants in Russia display their goods to purchasers from far-away Middle Eastern lands. The visitors have travelled over 3,000 kilometres to trade with the Vikings.

Russian village

slaves for sale

Muslim traders

beads

furs

walrus ivory

wax

Viking brooches

Viking merchants who have travelled to Russia

Churches and raiders

The Saxons worshipped pagan gods. In AD 597, the Pope in Rome sent missionaries to teach them about the Christian faith. Priests also went to England from the Celtic church in Ireland.

Saxon kings gave generously to support priests, monks and nuns. In turn, the churches encouraged learning and the arts. Church buildings were decorated with gold and silver crosses, hand-painted manuscripts, books in jewelled covers and embroidered robes. These rich, beautiful buildings were an easy target for Vikings to attack. They made their first raid on an English monastery at Lindisfarne in AD 793.

This gold shrine contained precious holy relics. It was seized by Viking raiders from a church in Ireland and carried back home to the Viking lands.

church

Viking ships

Viking raiders

precious gold cross

sword

helmet

Holy book

shield

Anglo Saxon chroniclers, describing Viking raids, wrote "Never before has such terror appeared in Britain."

Viking
ship

farm
animals

Viking
settlers

Viking settlers came to
England hoping to find better
land and a warmer climate
than in their homelands.
At first, there was fighting,
but eventually Saxon and
Viking people lived peacefully
together.

household
goods

Saxons
watching
on shore

Soldiers and settlers

The first Viking raiders were soon followed by a larger Viking army. They landed in southern England, and set up a camp there. They used this camp as a base for making raids. Later, the Vikings demanded money from the Saxon kings—or else they would attack their lands. The money was called Danegeld.

Other Vikings invaded the north of England. Vikings and Saxons fought fiercely, but finally, they made peace. The Vikings ruled in the north and east, called the Danelaw, while Saxon kings governed the rest of Britain. After AD 865, Viking families settled in the Danelaw, and Viking kings made their home in York.

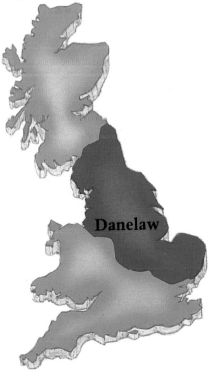

This map shows the Danelaw: the English lands where the Vikings ruled. Many Danelaw villages still have Viking names, given to them by the Viking settlers who came to live there.

Danelaw

This panel from a little box, carved out of ivory, shows scenes from Saxon legends. Like the Vikings, Saxon people could be fierce fighters. The box was made in the north of England around AD 700.

A wooden church in Norway, built around AD 1200, at the end of Viking times.
By then, the Vikings had become Christians.

This huge cross stands in a churchyard in Gosforth, in Cumbria. It shows how local people and Viking craftsmen worked together. Although it is a Christian monument, it is decorated with pagan Viking designs.

Two cultures meet

Saxon and Viking people were very different. They spoke different languages and had different customs and beliefs. Their craftsmen worked in different styles, following different traditions.

The earlier Viking kings were war-leaders who admired loyalty and bravery. Later Viking kings were strong rulers and wise law-makers. Saxon kings could also be warlike, but they valued art, religion, learning, good laws and peace.

In England, Saxon and Viking cultures met and mixed together. Vikings learned about Christianity from Saxon bishops and kings. A new English language developed, using Saxon and Viking words. We still speak a version of this language today.

Part of a tapestry, showing three Viking gods. Pagan Viking beliefs survived for many years alongside the Vikings' new Christian faith.

What happened next?

While one Viking army was landing in England, other Viking troops were invading France. In AD 911, the French king agreed to let these Vikings settle on some of his land. They became known as 'Normans', that is, 'the men from the north'.

In AD 1047, Duke William, a brave and daring Norman soldier, took control of Norman lands in France. He hoped to become king of England, as well. William invaded England in 1066. He knew that Harold, the Saxon king, was weak after fighting the Vikings. His Norman troops won a great victory at Hastings, where Harold was killed. Duke William, now called 'the Conquerer', became king. In England, it was the end of Saxon and Viking power.

The Normans made treaties with Saxon kings. King Edward the Confessor, pictured here ruled the Saxon lands from 1042-66. He was an ally of Duke William.

The two pictures on this page come from the Bayeux Tapestry, an enormous cloth embroidered by Norman women around AD 1100. It tells the story of the Norman conquest of England. Here, you can see Norman soldiers arriving at Hastings. The Norman warships are very like the Viking ship shown on page 15.

Another scene from the Bayeux Tapestry. Saxon and Norman soldiers are fighting with swords, spears and battle-axes. Harold, the last Saxon king of England, was killed by an arrow fired by a Norman soldier.

How do we know?

Many different types of evidence survive to tell us about life in Viking and Saxon times. How many have you spotted in this book?

There are carvings and statues (on pages 7 and 12), weapons and armour (pages 7 and 8), ships (page 15), tapestries (page 25), coins and metalwork (pages 16 and 18), manuscripts (page 18) and jewels (page 8). Viking poets and Saxon writers have also left us descriptions of events as they remembered them.

You can see other kinds of evidence on these pages, like burials and reconstructions. Both have been used by historians to discover more about life in Britain at the time when Vikings and Saxons came face to face.

This modern reconstruction of a Viking ship was made to help find out about how the Vikings sailed. Copies of Viking ships have proved that the Vikings were clever at designing boats to sail in rough, icy seas.

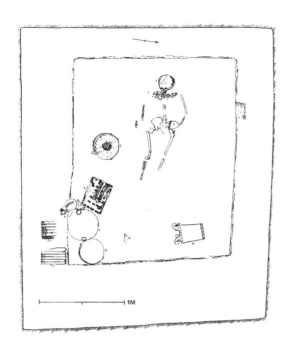

This drawing of a woman's grave from the Viking trading town of Birka was made by a modern archaeologist. It shows the woman's skeleton and some of the valuable objects buried with her.

Gold brooches like these were found in many Viking graves. They were buried with dead people, because the Vikings believed in life after death. Then, people would need all the goods they had treasured while they were alive.

Many fine English manuscripts have survived. This is a prayer-book. Manuscripts tell us about the wealth and learning of the Saxon Church, and about the skills of the monks who produced them. They also tell us about the beliefs of the wealthy Saxon men and women who paid for them.

Dates to remember

Vikings

AD 1066
Viking troops from Norway attack England, but are defeated by Saxon King Harold. Soon after, King Harold is killed by invading Normans. The Norman leader, William the Conquerer, becomes king of England.

AD 1000 (thereabouts)
Viking explorers reach Newfoundland in present-day Canada.

AD 911
Vikings settle in France. They are soon known as Normans (men from the north).

AD 866
Vikings set up a kingdom around York in northern England, called the Danelaw.

AD 865
Viking army spends winter in Britain.

AD 793
First Viking raid in Britain at Lindisfarne.

AD 2000

You were born

AD 1000

AD 400

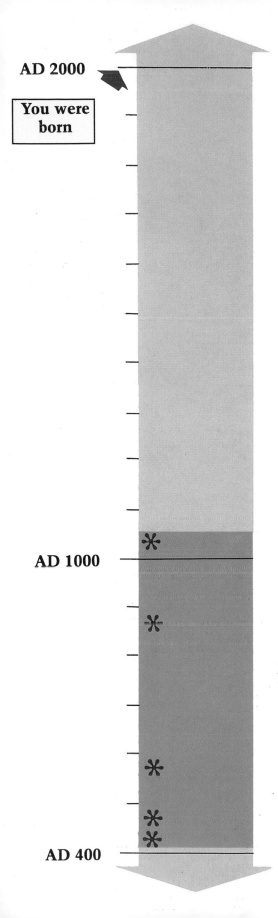

AD 2000

You were
born

AD 1000

AD 400

Saxons

AD 1066
Death of King Harold, the last Saxon king of England.

AD 871-889
Reign of King Alfred, Saxon king of Wessex (south-west England).
He defended England from Viking attack and encouraged religion and learning.

AD 597
St Augustine sent by the Pope to convert the Saxons in Britain to Christianity. Many Celtic people were already Christian. They had been converted by missionaries from Ireland.

AD 449
Traditional date of the first Saxon invasion of England (with their neighbours, the Angles and the Jutes). But nobody knows for certain.

AD 410
Last Roman troops leave Britain.

Words explained

Amber Shiny yellow 'stone' used in jewellery. Really the fossilised gum from pine trees.

Archaeologists People who study objects found in the ground to learn about the past.

Celtic people Settled in Britain after 800 BC and were invaded by the Romans in AD 43.

Chroniclers People who wrote about events as they happened.

Culture A way of life, including religion, music, art and poetry.

Ermine Fur from the white, winter coat of the stoat, a small animal, like a weasel.

Hawk A bird of prey which can be trained to hunt.

Ivory From elephant and walrus tusks. Used for jewellery and decorative objects.

Manuscripts Handwritten documents, often decorated with beautiful pictures.

Missionaries People who tell others about a new religion.

Navigation Science of steering a boat across the open sea.

Pagan Not Christian, and not belonging to any other major world faith.

Plunder Goods stolen in a raid.

Prow Front end of a boat.

Salting Preserving food by soaking in salty water.

Scribes People who wrote and decorated manuscripts.

Shifts Long, loose dresses.

Smoking Preserving food by hanging it over a smoky fire.

Stern Back end of a boat.

Tapestry Cloth with pictures or patterns woven or stitched in.

Uninhabited Where no-one lives.

Valhalla A place for dead heroes in Viking myths.

Walrus An animal like a seal which has two long teeth called tusks.

Exploration

Tony D. Triggs

Wayland

Titles in the series

Cover illustrations: *Background* Map showing Drake's circumnavigation of the globe. *Inset* Sir Francis Drake.

First published in 1993 by Wayland (Publishers) Ltd
61 Western Road, Hove, East Sussex BN3 1JD

© Copyright 1993 Wayland (Publishers) Ltd

Editor: Cath Senker
Designer: John Christopher
Consultant: Linda Goddard, Primary History Advisory Teacher, Runnymede Staff Development Centre, Surrey

British Library Cataloguing in Publication Data

Triggs, Tony D.
  Exploration. – (Tudors and Stuarts series)
  I. Title II. Series
  910.94

ISBN 0-7502-0688-8

Typeset by Strong Silent Type
Printed and bound by B.P.C.C. Paulton Books, Great Britain

Picture acknowledgements
British Library 21 (below); British Museum 21 (above); ET Archive 22 (below); 23 (both); Eye Ubiquitous (J Northover) 5, 27 (below); Michael Holford 4,12,14,15,17,22 (above), 25 (below); Mansell Collection *cover* (background) 7,13 (below), 16 (above) 24,25 (above); Mary Evans (Explorer) 8, 28; Mary Rose Trust 10 (both), 11 (above); National Maritime Museum 13 (above); National Portrait Gallery *cover* (inset), title page, 19; The Trustees of the National Museums of Scotland 1993 11 (below); Science Museum 6; Ronald Sheridan Pictures 20; Paul Smith 26; Wayland 27 (above) Artwork: Peter Bull 6,16,24.

Notes for teachers

Exploration includes a wide range of exciting sources including contemporary maps, artefacts, paintings and drawings.
This book:

◆ explains why Europeans explorers went on voyages and how the improved design of ships and navigational equipment enabled them to travel long distances.

◆ helps the reader to understand how we use clues from the past to learn about how people lived then.

◆ Primary sources provoke discussion of the encounters between the European explorers and the native American people.

Contents

The search for spice

The Tudor kings and queens ruled England and Wales from 1485 to 1603, and the Stuarts ruled England, Scotland and Wales from 1603 to 1714. During the time of the Tudors and Stuarts, European explorers went on many voyages to other lands.

The map below was drawn in the late fifteenth century. It shows all the places that people in Europe knew about. Try to pick out Europe, Asia and Africa. People in Europe did not know about North and South America, so these places did not appear on their maps.

A map of the world which was drawn in the late fifteenth century.

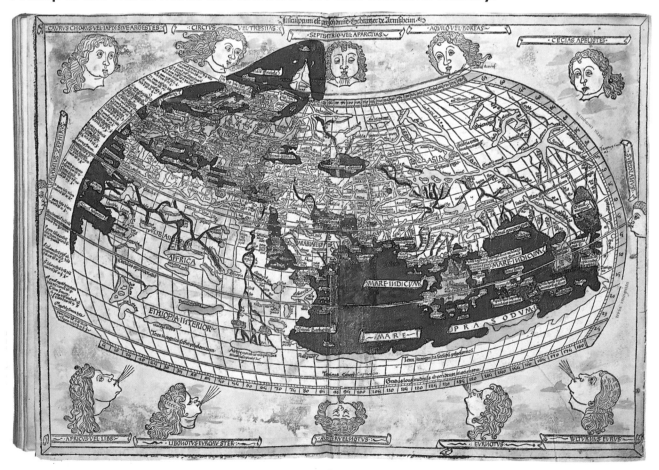

Spices from all around the world are sold in Britain today. How do you think merchants transport them? Why do you think we need spice less than people did in Tudor and Stuart times?

The need for spice

Spice was very important to the people of Europe, as it stopped their meat from going bad. If it did go bad, spice helped to hide the unpleasant taste.

Spices such as cinnamon, ginger and cloves came from some far-away islands which Europeans called the Indies. Spice merchants faced a very difficult journey when they went to the Indies and returned with heavy sacks of spice. Storms sometimes sank their ships at sea, and robbers often attacked them on land.

Finding an easier route

Some merchants in the fifteenth century thought that the world was flat. Others knew it was round, and many explorers agreed with them. They thought that merchants could reach the Indies by sailing across the Atlantic Ocean.

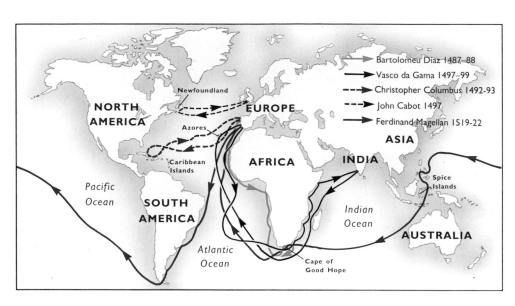

Bartolomeu Diaz 1487–88
Vasco da Gama 1497–99
Christopher Columbus 1492-93
John Cabot 1497
Ferdinand Magellan 1519-22

NORTH AMERICA
Newfoundland
EUROPE
Azores
Caribbean Islands
AFRICA
INDIA
Spice Islands
ASIA
Pacific Ocean
SOUTH AMERICA
Indian Ocean
AUSTRALIA
Atlantic Ocean
Cape of Good Hope

Some explorers went East to reach the Indies and others went West.

A model of Columbus' ship, the *Santa Maria*.

Christopher Columbus

In 1492 an Italian sailor called Christopher Columbus set off from Spain and sailed across the Atlantic Ocean. He wanted to get to the Indies, but he reached another land instead. If you look at the map above you can see the land Columbus found. No one in Europe had heard of this land, and the people who lived there had not heard of Europe!

Clues in pictures

Why were fifteenth century explorers able to sail so far? It was partly because they had learned to build better ships than the people who had lived before.

Shipbuilders at work.

This picture from 1493 gives clues about how ships were built at that time. You can see quite a lot of the tools that were used, and perhaps you can pick out the man in charge.

What was Columbus like?

Many people in Europe think that Columbus was a clever sailor but others point to his faults and mistakes. He thought he had found a new way to Asia but he had really found America. His men and other sailors from Europe treated the peoples who lived there badly.

At first Columbus made friends with the native Americans. Perhaps he was trying to gain their trust in order to trick them.

There are several statues of Columbus in Europe. Read this chapter and decide whether you think he deserves to be treated like a hero.

Here are some of the things Columbus wrote about the native Americans:

" I gave them red caps, glass beads and many other little things, and they brought us parrots and balls of cotton and spears and many other things.

They seemed to me a poor people. They were all naked as the day they were born. I showed them a sword and they took it by the edge and cut themselves out of ignorance, for they don't have anything made of iron.

They would make fine servants, and when I leave I will bring back half a dozen [six] of them. With fifty men we could overcome all the natives and make them do what we wanted. "

In the seventeenth century a Spaniard called Bartolomé de las Casas wrote about some of the things Columbus had said and done. He said:

" Columbus had no idea of what was right and wrong when he said he could bring all the natives to Spain or use them as servants in their own country. "

This shows that Columbus was interested in other things as well as spice. People in Europe were beginning to think of farming the land in other countries and using the native people as slaves. They began to do this from the start of the sixteenth century (a few years after Columbus' voyage).

Native Americans did not write, so we do not have any books which say what they thought of Columbus. Maybe you can imagine how they felt.

Tools and equipment

The *Mary Rose* was a Tudor warship. In 1545 it sank suddenly in Portsmouth harbour. No one is sure what made it sink. In 1982 archaeologists raised it from the mud at the bottom of the water and put it on display in a museum. They also displayed the tools and other things they had found inside the ship.

The objects above were found in the wreck of the *Mary Rose*.

The wreck of the *Mary Rose* in the museum.

Clues in objects

The objects in the picture above were found in the *Mary Rose*. They help to show what life on Tudor ships was like. The whistle was probably used to give signals. Perhaps it told the sailors when to start and stop their jobs. The whistle and comb are made of wood. Try to decide what the other things are and what they are made of. (Answers p.31)

Death at sea

Many men died at sea. The *Mary Rose* contained the skeletons of men who drowned when it sank. Men who sailed on warships often died in battles, and others were wounded. A doctor's tools and jars of ointment were found in the wreck of the *Mary Rose*. They show that the doctor was expecting to treat some serious injuries after a battle.

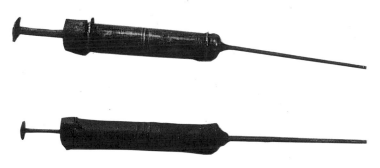

The doctor's syringes from the *Mary Rose*.

Here is a model of the *Great Michael*, a powerful warship launched off Scotland in 1511.

Dangers at sea

Women rarely went to sea. It was felt that life on a ship was too harsh and unpleasant for them. It was often too harsh for the men as well. Even when they were cold and ill they had to work extremely hard. Pulling on ropes rubbed the skin off their hands. Some men died from the terrible whippings their captains gave them to make them work harder.

If you look at this painting carefully you can see sailors in the ship's rigging (the ropes and sails).

Horrible falls

Many sailors died in accidents on board their ships. The wind and the waves shook their ships so much that some men had horrible falls from the rigging. They hit the deck or disappeared into the sea below, where there were hungry sharks.

Scurvy

Some sailors died of a disease called scurvy, which is caused by eating a very poor diet. They could not take much fresh food to sea because it would have gone bad too quickly. For months, sailors had almost nothing to eat except dry, salted meat and hard biscuits. When they caught scurvy, their gums bled, their teeth fell out, and sores and lumps appeared on their bodies. The sailors needed to reach land quickly to find some fresh fruit and vegetables. If they were far from land, the sick men died.

A ship's biscuit.

Fights

Explorers' ships did not take part in big battles, but some men died in fights with explorers from other countries. Others died fighting the people who lived in the countries they found, but they usually won these fights quite easily. (To find out why they usually won, look at chapter 3 again and think about what Columbus said.)

1492
Columbus reaches America.

1520
The Spaniards start to colonize the American mainland.

1545
The *Mary Rose* sinks.

Archaeologists sometimes find sailors' skeletons, and the skeletons help to show which diseases they suffered from. How could you tell if a sailor had suffered from scurvy?

Monsters

Sailors believed in monsters called sea serpents, which could coil their snake-like bodies round a ship and pull it to the bottom of the sea.

Sailors thought there were sea serpents in the sea.

Finding the way

Tudor explorers did not have maps of the new places they were going to. It was hundreds of years since Vikings from Norway and Denmark had crossed the Atlantic Ocean. The Vikings had not left any maps so the explorers had to draw their own.

A board with pegs. Every half an hour a sailor put in a peg to show which way the ship had sailed.

Using the sun and the stars

Explorers checked their direction by studying the sun and the stars. As they crossed the Atlantic Ocean, they knew that the sun would always be in the south at midday. At night they knew that a star called the Pole Star would be in the north.

Working out speed

It was hard for sailors to work out how fast they were going. They sometimes took a length of rope to the front of the ship and threw one end of it into the sea. There was nothing to make the end of the rope move along with the ship, so it just stayed still and floated.

The sailors noted down how long it took for the ship to go right past the rope. This helped them to work out how fast the ship was going.

Sailors in the sixteenth century sometimes tied a log to the end of the rope. The log helped to make it float and show up easily. The sailors also tied knots in the rope, and they counted how many knots the ship passed in a certain time. The captain then made notes in a special book called a log book. Captains still keep a log book, and they still give the speed of their ship in knots.

An hourglass, a simple kind of clock.

An hourglass

Sailors sometimes used an hourglass. It worked like an egg timer. It took an hour for the sand to go from the top half into the bottom half. Sailors used it like a clock.

They needed to know how much time had passed to work out how far their ship had gone.

Drake sails round the world

In the 1560s, when he was young, the English sailor Francis Drake went to sea with his cousins, John and William Hawkins. They were merchants and they grew quite rich. Later, Drake sailed right round the world. He was one of the first people to do so.

Drake and his cousins took finished goods, such as clothing, from England and sold them in Africa. Then they took people from Africa and sold them as slaves to the Spaniards who had settled in the Caribbean.

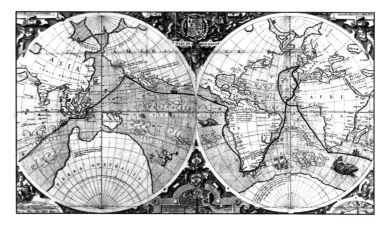

This map appeared in 1589. It shows Drake's journey round the world. A line has been added to make the route show up.

Finally, they came home from the Caribbean with sugar and cotton to sell in England.

Sailing round the world

Queen Elizabeth I, who ruled England from 1558–1603, wanted to get her revenge on the King of Spain for Spanish attacks on English ships. She asked Drake to help her.

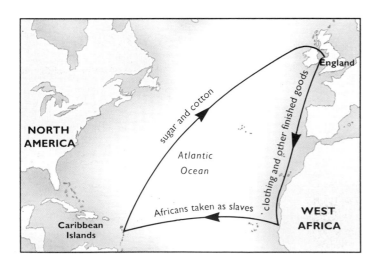

This modern map shows how Drake bought and sold goods and people. Are modern traders allowed to sell people?

In 1580 Drake headed south and went round the tip of South America. Once he was in the Pacific Ocean he behaved like a pirate, robbing Spanish ships and filling his own ship with treasure. After sailing across the Pacific Ocean, he came home along the western coast of Africa. He had gone round the world!

Drake used an instrument called a compass to help him find his way. The Chinese had invented compasses over a thousand years earlier, but they had only been used in Europe for about two hundred years.

A compass works because it has a magnet inside it. The magnet is carefully balanced so that it turns very easily. A magnet which is free to turn always points to the north.

Making a compass

Compasses are still used today, and it is easy to make one. You will need a needle, a magnet, a small, flat piece of wood or cork, and a bowl of water. Be careful with the needle.

A compass like the one Drake used.

What to do:

1. Make sure the needle sticks to the magnet.
2. Stroke the needle with the magnet several times. This turns the needle into another, tiny magnet.
3. Move the first magnet out of the way.
4. Put the piece of wood or cork on the water and rest the needle on it.
5. One end of the needle should point to the north and the other end should point to the south.

Try to think of a way of checking whether your compass is working. Could Drake have checked his compass in the same way?

A rogue or a gentleman?

Queen Elizabeth admired Drake – she knighted him and his name became Sir Francis Drake. But there is evidence that he was a violent man, and a thief.

A fine English gentleman

Look at the picture on the right. One of Queen Elizabeth's favourite artists painted this portrait of Francis Drake. What is Drake's hand resting on? Why do you think the artist has included it in the picture?

A thief and a rogue

We can learn a lot about the past from things that were written at the time. A man called Richard Hakluyt wrote about famous voyages. The following passage comes from what he wrote about Drake:

" *They found a Spanish ship off the coast of Chile; and the men on the ship, thinking Drake's men were Spaniards, welcomed them with a drum and a giant barrel of wine. But then one of Drake's men punched the Spanish pilot in the face and called him a dog... Drake captured the ship and chained the men up. Then he went on shore and robbed the houses. He went into a warehouse and took the wine. He also took the silver dishes and the altar cloth from a little church.* "

Different clues

The portrait makes Drake look very fine and respectable but Hakluyt makes him sound greedy and nasty. When we study history we have to look at lots of clues and then decide things for ourselves.

A portrait of Francis Drake.

Sir Walter Raleigh

The English explorer Sir Walter Raleigh lived in England at the time of Queen Elizabeth I and King James I. In 1595 he explored parts of South America looking for a rich and beautiful land with a city called El Dorado. He had heard that the city was built of gold.

Stories of treasure

The peoples of South America had a lot of treasure, but Raleigh found very little of it. He heard many stories about it, but that was all. One story told of a king who ate from dishes made of gold and silver. He also had sticks of gold that were made to look like firewood.

Another story told of people who shone because they were covered in gold.

According to Raleigh:

" They rub their naked bodies with sap to make them sticky. Then their servants take hollow sticks and blow powdered gold all over them until they are shining from head to foot. "

Treasure made of gold from South America.

Raleigh found pineapples in South America.

Better than gold!

Raleigh did not find El Dorado but he brought back potatoes, bananas, pineapples and other foods which people in Britain had never seen.

Life near the River Orinoco

Raleigh wrote about the people who lived by the River Orinoco in South America:

"*In summer some of them have huts on the ground; but in winter the River Orinoco rises thirty feet* [nine metres], *flooding the places where they live and forcing them to live in the trees.*"

By saying this, Raleigh made these people sound rather silly and helpless.

Perhaps he did not realize how clever they really were. They were used to the floods and built themselves excellent homes in the tree-tops. They were also good at catching the fish that swam just below their homes.

Raleigh helped Europeans to think that they were better than the people they met in far-away countries. This allowed the Europeans to treat those people badly without feeling ashamed.

This picture shows what people did when the rivers in South America flooded.

Colonies in America

There were many different peoples living in North and South America when the Europeans arrived. The Spanish, Portuguese and English explorers fought these peoples so they could take the land and riches for themselves. The parts where people from Europe settled were known as colonies.

A Native American village in North America. This picture by an English painter shows how the people lived before the Europeans arrived.

A map of the coast of Virginia, showing the dangers for the settlers.

The Roanoke colony

In 1585 Raleigh started a colony at Roanoke, in Virginia (now part of the USA). At that time the land belonged to the Pamlico people. Raleigh's colony did not last long, for the European farmers disappeared. Perhaps the Pamlico killed them to get their land back. The map gives a clue to other problems the settlers faced. Look at it carefully and try to think what some of the problems were. (See p.31 for ideas.)

The Pilgrim Fathers

In 1620 a group of English people who had been living in Holland decided to set up a colony in North America. They did this because other people in Europe did not like their Puritan religious beliefs. The group sailed to England, where more people joined them. Then they sailed to Massachusetts. Their colony did well, and people in the USA sometimes call them the Pilgrim Fathers. Pilgrims are people who go on a very long journey because of what they believe, but why do you think Americans call these settlers 'Fathers'?

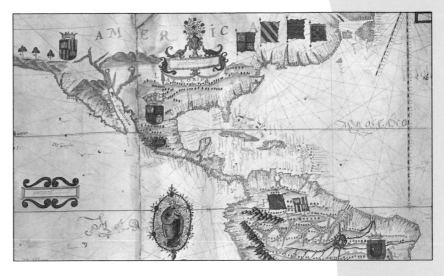

A map of North and South America in 1623, showing the colonies.

The Pilgrim Fathers leave for America.

Flags and shields

This map was drawn in 1623, after people from Europe had set up many colonies in North and South America, ill-treating and often killing the people who had lived there before. The flags and shields on the map show where the colonies were.

In 1698 people from Scotland tried to set up a colony at Darien, in what is now Colombia, South America, but most of the colonists died from diseases.

Timeline

1560s
Drake makes merchant voyages with John and William Hawkins.

1577–1580
Drake sails round the world.

1585
Raleigh tries to start a colony in North America.

1595
Raleigh's expedition to South America.

1620
The Pilgrim Fathers set up a colony in Massachusetts.

23

A new way to Asia?

Columbus had never reached Asia.
Drake had got there by taking a very
long and difficult route around the tip of
South America. In Stuart times, people
tried to find an easier route.

**(Right) Willem Barents, a
Dutch explorer, died of cold
on an expedition in 1597.**

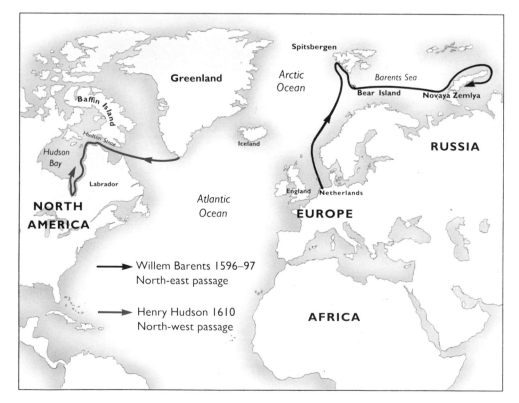

A modern map to show the search for new ways to Asia.

Blocked by ice

Some explorers tried to
reach Asia by going round
the north of what is now
Canada. They called this
route 'the north-west
passage'. Other explorers
tried to reach Asia by
going round the north of
Europe. They called this
route 'the north-east
passage'. Both routes
were blocked by the ice
around the North Pole.

A medal (above), and a document (below right) called a charter. King Charles II issued them when the Hudson Bay Company was formed in 1670.

Henry Hudson

Hudson was an English explorer who worked for a Dutch company. He tried to reach Asia by both routes, but frozen seas stopped him. However, in 1610 he discovered a huge bay in northern Canada. It is called Hudson Bay in memory of him.

Hudson Bay became a very important centre for trade. People who lived around the bay trapped animals and sold the furs to merchants from Europe.

The Hudson Bay Company

European kings and queens encouraged exploration and trade, because traders had to pay them taxes. Trading was done by companies such as the Hudson Bay Company. The king or queen made an agreement with each new company. The agreement said what the company was allowed to sell and how much tax it would have to pay. They wrote their agreement down in a charter.

From past to present

The Tudor and Stuart explorers gave the people of Europe new foods, new land, new ideas and new power.

1992 was the 500th anniversary of Columbus' voyage to America. Some people in Europe and the USA held celebrations. Others, mainly in South America, were very angry and said that explorers like Columbus, Drake and Raleigh were evil men. They pointed out that the European explorers and settlers had killed other peoples, or used them as slaves.

Many of the black people who live in the USA and Caribbean today are descended from Africans. The Africans were taken there by men like Drake to work as slaves on white people's farms.

These people from Guatemala in Central America are protesting against what the European explorers and settlers did to their people.

Tobacco

Raleigh and other explorers saw native Americans smoking dried tobacco leaves and they brought some home for Europeans to try. At first they thought that smoking was good for them. Now we know it is very harmful, and people who smoke find it hard to stop.

Most of the tobacco sold in Britain is still grown in the USA.

This cartoon about smoking tobacco appeared in Stuart times.

Fruit and vegetables from a supermarket. Which of these foods would we have to go without if explorers had not discovered them in America?

Answer: banana, sweet corn, pineapple, potato.

Timeline

1480	1500	1520	1540	1560	1580

Tudors

| 1485 HENRY VII | 1509 HENRY VIII | | 1547 EDWARD VI / 1553 MARY TUDOR / 1558 ELIZABETH I | | |

1480–1500	1500–1520	1520–1540	1540–1560	1560–1580	1580–1600
1492 Columbus sails to America.	1500–1547 Sheep farmers enclose common land.	1520 The Spaniards start to colonize the American mainland.	1543 Vesalius publishes his book about the human body.	1560s Drake makes merchant voyages with John and William Hawkins.	1587 Mary Queen of Scots is executed.
	1509 Cabot tries to sail round the north of Canada.	1535 Henry VIII becomes Head of the Church in England and Wales.	1545 The *Mary Rose* sinks.	1567 As a Catholic, Mary Queen of Scots flees from Scotland but is imprisoned in England.	1588 The Spanish Armada is defeated.
	1511 The *Great Michael* is launched.	1536 Anne Boleyn is put to death.	1547–1553 Protestants are persecuted and put to death.		1595 Raleigh explores South America.
		1539 Henry VIII has the monasteries destroyed.	1547–1553 Many schools and colleges are built.	1577 Drake sets off on his voyage around the world.	1590–1616 Shakespeare writes his plays.
			1549 Robert Kett leads a rebellion in Norfolk.		

1600   1620   1640   1660   1680   1700

Stuarts

1603 JAMES I (JAMES VI OF SCOTLAND)

1625 CHARLES I

1649–1660 COMMONWEALTH
1653 OLIVER CROMWELL
1658 RICHARD CROMWELL

1660 CHARLES II

1685 JAMES II
1688 WILLIAM III & MARY II

1702–1714 ANNE

1600–1620	1620–1640	1640–1660	1660–1680	1680–1700	1700–1710
1605 The Gunpowder Plot.	**1628** William Harvey describes how blood goes round the body.	**1642** The Civil War begins.	**1665** The Plague.	**1690** The Battle of the Boyne.	**1707** England and Scotland are officially united.
1607 Henry Hudson sets off to explore the coast of northern Canada.	**1630–1641** Charles I rules without Parliament.	**1646** Charles I is captured and imprisoned.	**1666** The Great Fire of London.	**1694** Mary II dies.	
1610 Hudson discovers a huge bay in northern Canada that is named after him.		**1649** Charles I is executed.	**1670** The Hudson Bay Company is founded.	**1680–1695** Henry Purcell writes his music.	
1620 The Pilgrim Fathers go to America.		**1649 1660** England and Wales are ruled without a king or queen.	**1660–1669** Samuel Pepys writes his diary.	**1698** Scots set up Darien colony in South America, which fails.	
			1660–1685 Hooke and Newton study light and gravity.		
			Sir Christopher Wren designs many new buildings.		
			1670–1689 Aphra Behn writes her lively plays.		

Glossary

Archaeologists People who study the past from remains.

Charter A legal document containing an agreement about land or trade.

Colony A place where a group of people from a different country settle.

Descendants The living relatives of people who have died.

Indies The name Europeans used in Tudor and Stuart times to describe the lands in the east, such as India, China, Japan and the Spice Islands.

Knighted Given the title 'Sir' by a queen or king for service to the country.

Knot A measure of speed used by sailors, equal to about 1.85 km per hour.

Log book The book in which a ship's captain makes notes about a voyage.

Merchant Someone who buys and sells goods.

Native Americans The people already living in America when the Europeans went there.

Puritan A very strict Christian who prays a lot and avoids fun and entertainment.

Revenge Taking revenge is when you hurt someone to pay them back for a bad thing they have done to you.

Rogue Someone who cannot be trusted.

Route The way from one place to another.

Spices Strong-tasting substances used in cooking to give food a good flavour.

Syringes Doctors' needles.

Books to read

Easy books

Anderson, D. *The Spanish Armada* (Macdonald, 1988)

Carter, M., Culpin, C. and Kinloch, N. *Past into Present 2: 1400 – 1700* (Collins Educational, 1990)

Kelly, T. *Children in Tudor England* (Thornes and Hulton, 1987)

Middleton, H. *Everyday Life in the Sixteenth Century* (Macdonald, 1982)

Triggs, T.D. *Tudor Britain* (Wayland, 1989)

Triggs, T.D. *Tudor and Stuart Times* (Folens, 1992)

Wood, T. *The Stuarts* (Ladybird, 1991)

Books for older readers

Koning, H. *Columbus: His Enterprise* (Latin American Bureau, 1991)

Linnell, N. and Postgate, O. *Columbus: The Triumphant Failure* (Grisewood and Dempsey, 1991)

Morrison, I. *'Mary Rose' : Her Wreck and Rescue* (Lutterworth, 1988)

Reische, D. *Founding the American Colonies* (Watts, 1989)

Tames, R. *Exploring Other Civilizations* (Thornes and Hulton, 1987)

Williams, B. *Voyages of Discovery* (Cherrytree, 1989)

Places to visit

The *Great Michael*,
National Trust for Scotland,
Falkland, Fife, Scotland

The *Mary Rose* exhibition,
Portsmouth, Hampshire

The National Maritime Museum,
Greenwich, London

Answers to questions:
p.10: The rosary beads are made of boxwood (wood from a box tree); whistle – ash wood; sundial – boxwood; dice – ivory; thimble – brass; clasp – silver; purse-hanger – copper alloy (copper mixed with other metals); knife handle – copper alloy and wood; tokens – one is brass, one is copper alloy; comb – boxwood; seal – boxwood.
p.22: There are dangerous sea creatures. Ships might be wrecked on one of the islands.

Index

Words in **bold** are subjects shown in pictures as well as in the text.